# IGGLESDEN'S KENT
## ~c.1900~

First published in Great Britain in 2024
by
Contemporary Watercolours (Oakweald) Ltd

Downsview,
Pett Lane,
Charing,
Kent
TN27 0DL

07958 762222
malcolmchorton@gmail.com

ISBN 978-19 068635823

No part of this book may be reproduced in any form without the permission of thepublisher except for quotation of brief passages in criticism.

Copyright for the text is reserved by Malcolm Horton

Historical Consultants:
Dave Fletcher and Peter Leach - Oxney Local History Group
Colin Young - Tenterden History Group
Robin Wilkins - Tenterden Museum
Andrew Richardson - Archaeologist

Layout:
Printcom.co.uk Ltd

Printed by:
Lightning Source UK,
Milton Keynes

# CONTENTS

5    I - Introduction

7    II - Sir Charles Igglesden

14   III - Ebony - Charles Igglesden - 1900

17   IV - Stone-in-Oxney - Charles Igglesden - 1923

29   V - Wittersham - Charles Igglesden - 1923

47   VI - Oxney - Malcolm Horton Revisit - 2024

# I
# INTRODUCTION

In 2018 I wrote a biography of Sir Charles Igglesden, a man of many talents, who died in 1949. He is chiefly remembered for his series of essays "A Saunter through Kent with Pen and Pencil".

The first essay appeared in the Kentish Express on 28th April 1899 and featured the village of Kennington, now a suburb of Ashford. The series of essays, ran until 1944 and in that forty five year period Igglesden visited 242 villages. All were illustrated by Xavier Willis. Such was their popularity that each year's village visits were issued in hard back form.

In the foreword to my biography of Sir Charles Igglesden, the distinguished historian and writer Martin Latham, spoke of the essays in the following terms:

"These unjustly neglected essays or Saunters through Kent villages, are casement windows onto a lost World, before the age of speeding cars and over lit streets, when Kent still moved to the rhythm of horse hoof and steam train. The superb pen and ink sketches by Xavier Willis complement Igglesden's painterly prose".

We have decided to produce booklets of Igglesden's original essays to selected villages, followed up by a visit to the villages in 2024, over 100 years later, to see how they have changed.

Also included is a potted biography of Sir Charles taken from the full biography "Sauntering through Kent"

Welcome to the picturesque world of Charles Igglesden's Saunters.

Malcolm Horton

## II
## Sir Charles Igglesden
### A True Man of Kent

On the 22nd April 1899, there appeared in The Kentish Express under the heading "A Saunter Through Kent with Pen and Pencil", an article about Kennington, "a picturesque parish not two miles distant from Ashford". The paper announced that this was to be the first in a series of articles describing the villages of Kent.

The author of this first article although, unnamed, was Charles Igglesden (1861-1949) who was Editor of The Kentish Express and the illustrator was Xavier Willis, the paper's resident artist. Little could they have expected that the series would run for over 45 years, with the same men wielding pen and pencil.

By the time the last article appeared in October 1944 their peregrinations around Kent had covered 242 villages and towns. Such was the demand, that the articles were, each year, published in hard back book form and altogether 34 volumes were produced between 1900 and 1946.

Charles Igglesden had been appointed Editor of The Kentish Express at the tender age of twenty-three in 1884 and altogether served in that post for over 64 years. His peers in Fleet Street and beyond recognised that he was an exceptional journalist and a man of some political acumen, when in 1927, they appointed him President of the Institute of Journalists (the oldest newspaper society in the world). This was quickly followed in 1928 by a Knighthood for services to journalism.

However, journalism and the "Saunter" books, represented only two facets of his life, for he was a man of many parts. He was an eclectic mix of interests and abilities which included sporting prowess, literary distinction as an author and novelist, archaeology and chess. Above all he was a politician and man of public affairs, who was part of Kent public life for over fifty years. He was an Alderman on Kent County Council for over forty years, and Deputy Lord Lieutenant of Kent.

Charles Igglesden was born in Ashford on the 7th February 1861, the second son of Henry Igglesden, who had founded the Kentish Express in 1855. Henry's father John Bourn Igglesden was a partner with his brother

Benjamin in the family bakery business located in Market Place, Dover. It had been founded by their father and mother John and Amy Igglesden in 1788. The Igglesdens were a well-respected Dover family, devout Baptist and a cornerstone of the local community. However, tragedy struck in 1836 when John Bourn died suddenly from a heart disease at the young age of forty, to be followed three years later by his wife Elizabeth.

Henry and his brother John, now orphans, were cared for separately by friends. Henry was cared for by John and Eliza May. John May was a printer and it was no surprise that Henry became apprenticed to him. Once he finished his apprenticeship Henry moved to Ashford and married a local girl Sarah Ann in 1851, and set up a printing business in Ashford High Street.

In 1855, in the wake of the government's abolition of stamp duty on newspapers, he took a big gamble and founded Kent's first penny Newspaper The Ashford and Alfred News. It was a twice weekly newspaper published on Saturday and Tuesday and although a risky venture, it paid off handsomely. Henry had perceived that there was a growing demand from an increasingly literate public for news of not only local affairs but also news of the wider world. Henry's paper had a Paris Newsletter reporting events in Europe. Jottings with pen and pencil reporting parliamentary affairs in London whilst alongside would be reports on local wheat prices and other farming matters.

Such was the widening appeal of the paper that it was not long before offices were opened in Maidstone, Canterbury, Folkestone and Hasting. In 1858 "The Ashford and Alfred News" became "The Kentish Express" to reflect its wider geographical significance. Interestingly the Alfred part of the original name related to a new housing development, built by the South Eastern Railway Works in 1850, for its employees called Alfred Town a mile to the east of Ashford in Willesborough.

Charles Igglesden was educated privately, firstly at home by tutors and then in Paris. A cosmopolitan formal education of this sort was most unusual and may have had something to do with the Kentish Express's Paris correspondent. Charles returned to England in 1878 and became a Cub reporter on his fathers' paper, taking a special interest in sports reporting, particularly cricket for which he developed a life-long passion. He was later to write a weekly cricket column under the pen name LBW.

His love of cricket dated back to 1871 when as a ten-year old he attended the world-famous Annual Canterbury Cricket Week, and was spotted by the legendary WG Grace having a knock about with some older lads. Using an oak tree as the wicket WG proceeded to give him his first cricket lesson. This was the beginning of a life-long friendship. Some years later in 1876 Charles was lucky enough to witness WG score 344 sublime runs at the same Canterbury Cricket Week playing for the MCC against Kent. It was the first triple century to be scored in First Class Cricket. The Annual Canterbury Cricket Week founded in 1842 is the oldest cricket festival in the world, and Charles Igglesden reported them for over fifty years. Charles became an accomplished cricketer himself playing for several local clubs and he regularly took parties of cricketers to play in France up until the First World War.

Cricket was not the only sport at which Charles excelled, he was also a first-class rugby player and represented Kent at Lawn Tennis twice being runner up in the County Singles Championship. By complete contrast he also represented Kent at Chess. He was also accomplished at Billiards twice beating Sir Arthur Conan Doyle in the final of the Authors Club Championship.

Charles was appointed Editor of the Kentish Express ahead of his older brother William, who also worked for the paper, and given his young age, twenty-three, he must have been quite exceptional. The Kentish Express grew from strength to strength under his Editorship, becoming well known for its forthright and incisive editorials, and by the 1890's attained a circulation of 35,000 a week. His father Henry maintained his connection with the paper as Chairman until his death in 1907.

The only blot on the landscape was in 1891 when there took place disastrous arson attack carried out by a disgruntled ex-employee. The offices an works of The Kentish Express in Park Street Ashford were completely destroye as was every piece of machinery and type. However, a Fleet Street Newspape The Daily Chronicle (later The New Chronicle) came to the rescue and printe The Kentish Express until new premises were built in the High Street a fe months later. Amazingly the paper appeared as usual the following Saturda The Daily Chronicle was Fleet Streets largest selling newspaper. The connectio with The Kentish Express was probably established in 1884 when they bot became founder members of The Institute of Journalist. A few years late Igglesden was offered the Editors Chair of The Daily Chronicle. He declined th offer preferring to stay close to his roots in his beloved Kentish countrysid Nevertheless, the offer of this prestigious job was a mark of the high regard i which he was held as a journalist by Fleet Street.

Not long after being appointed Editor of The Kentish Express Charle Igglesden had in 1885 married Ellen, daughter of George E Swatman a senic civil servant at the Admiralty. They had four sons who all worked for the Kentis Express at different times of their lives. They moved to Heathfield, an imposin residence on the Canterbury Road, just north of Ashford in 1908 and lived ther together for over thirty years before Lady Igglesdens death in 1939. Sir Charle died ten years later in 1949 to be succeeded by his son. Only three editors in 10 years and all Igglesdens!

In 1901 Charles Igglesden the author first made his appearance on th Literary Scene with publication by The Kentish Express of "The Demon Eleven" This work had been preceded by two local histories "History of the East Ken Volunteers" (1899) and "A History of Ashford Church" (1901). By 1907 he ha also published 7 volumes of his "Saunters" and this emboldened him to approacl a London publisher Simpkin Marshall to publish a volume of ten short storie called "Strad" which received very favourable reviews in the National Press. Th poet Matthew Arnold once said that journalism is literature in a hurry and thi became the case with Igglesdens literature In 1910 John Long o London published hi first full length nove "A Flutter with Fate followed by three mor romantic novel "Clouds" (1912) "Lav the Wrecker" (1914 and "The Crimsor Glow" (1918). All ha Kentish background with Hythe, Folkeston and Smeeth featured i

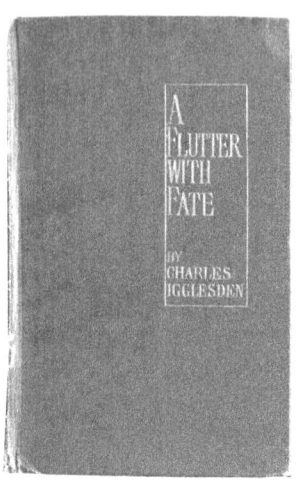

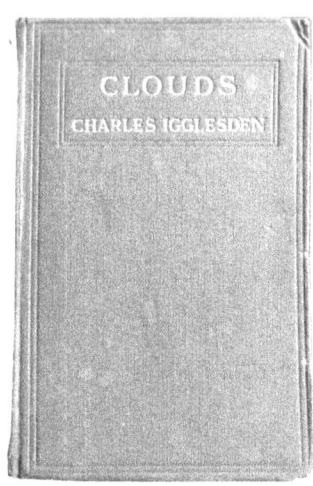

"Clouds". Romney Marsh and Littlestone in "Flutter with Fate" and The North Downs around Charing in the Crimson Glow. A later novel Downs Valley Farm {1940} again features he North Downs, but this time around Ashford Wye and Hastingleigh, just after the outbreak of the Second World War, and follows the romantic fortunes of two Land Girls (Woman's Land Army) who had been posted to the area. However, "Those Superstitions" published in 1931 in his most enduring publication after the "Saunters" series. As its title suggests it is a light-hearted investigation into the nature and origins of superstitions. Clearly much of the information was gleamed from his "Saunters Through Kent" series of books which is full of anecdotal tales and customs. It was considered to have been a serious enough work to have had the endorsement of the famous mystery writer Marjorie Bowen who wrote a lengthy foreword. "Those superstitions" is still held on over 130 public libraries throughout the world.

Two of Charles Igglesden's books in addition to the "Saunters" series were expanded versions of articles that had first appeared in The Kentish Express as first hand reports of official visits made overseas. The first published in 1916 was entitled "Out There", Impressions Of A Visit Under The Auspices Of The War Office. It came about partly as a result of an editorial Charles Igglesden had written in The Kentish Express on 25th September 1915, urging the government to shed more light on the true situation appertaining on the Western Front. He likened the government's claims that one Englishman was worth three Germans, as belonging to the Music Hall stage and was no longer believed by the average person. It coincided with demands from America that if Britain wanted their help more genuine newspaper reporting of the war should be forthcoming. It was therefore no great surprise that Kitchener sent a small party of journalists to the front in January 1916 to observe the situation. Charles Igglesden's inclusion in the party was ostensibly on the orders of Kitchener in order to write the script for a series of recruiting lectures. He was, after all, honorary recruiting officer for East Kent with the rank of Major. In the event the lectures did not take place because conscription was introduced. However, the visit provided excellent copy for a series of articles in The Kentish Express.

The second book published recording impressions of another official overseas visit was "A Mere Englishman in America". In 1928 a newly knighted Sir Charles Igglesden was invited to visit America as a guest of the Carnegie Peace Institute. He was included in an exclusive party of 14 British journalist to report back to the UK on how civilised America had become in a few short years, since the days of the Wild West. His companions included, The Editors of The London Times, The Daily Express, The Scotsman and The Belfast Telegraph.

Over a period of three months the journalist traversed America east from New York to California and west to east along the Mexican border to Washington.

Igglesden was distinctly underwhelmed by the "new" skyscrapers in New York, calling them claustrophobic, because they cut out the light and trapped the exhaust fumes, which caused sore throats. However, he was greatly impressed by the way the old Wild West towns such as Denver and Kansas transformed themselves in less than forty years into beautiful urban townships with wide boulevards and spacious parks.
He was somewhat disdainful about the average Americans obsession with material wealth and millionaire status as a sign of national pride.

Hollywood fascinated him where he noted that 50% of actors and directors were British especially after the advent of the Talkies. He met Douglas Fairbanks and his wife Mary Pickford; true Hollywood Royalty. Charlie Chaplin, in conversation, revealed himself to be a shrewd businessman. He greatly liked New Orleans real old world feel and buildings to match: Some were 200 years old! His favourite city was Washington the Presidential City. A very dignified place with no skyscrapers. It quite reminded him of home.

His parting thoughts were that greater understanding was needed between the two nations because after all they were like father and son who had grown apart because of 3,000 miles of ocean. Education was the answer, so that we might understand one another better.

After Charles's father Henry died in 1907 he seems to have increased his commitment to public service. He was elected to Kent County Council for West Ashford in 1907 and was an Alderman in 1914 until his death in 1949. He was for many years Chairman of the Kent National Health Insurance Committee {forerunner of The Area Health Authority and NHS}, and Vice Chairman of the Kent Higher Education Committee. He was a Fellow of the Society of Antiquaries and took a big interest in the Kent Archaeological Society. He served as President of The Association of Men of Kent and Kentish Men. He was also Chairman of the Kent County Industrial School, Chairman of the Ashford Division of Justices and as already mentioned he was Deputy Lord Lieutenant of Kent. In Freemasonry he was a Past Master of The Invicta Lodge and held the rank of Grand Assistant Directors of Ceremonies at the United Grand Lodge.

Sir Charles Igglesden FSA JP DL was a man of unbounding energy and wide ranging abilities who was still busy writing his fluent and often scathing editorials until shortly before his death in 1949 at the age of eighty-eight. However, the thirty-four volumes of "Saunters through Kent with Pen and Pencil" will be his lasting testimony. Although history has largely pigeonholed Igglesden as a light weight historian whose "Saunters Through Kent" books were not in the same scholarly league as Edward Hasted a century earlier. However, the Times Reviewer remarked that "Saunters" was an up to date Hasted history of Kent written in a more picturesque style. He was a storyteller whose unique local anecdotes are part of Kentish lore. And that is what the telling of historical tales has always traditionally been. What is more important, Igglesden idea was to captivate the imagination and communicate his love of history and the beauty of the Kentish countryside to a far wider audience than ever did the rather prosaic Hasted.

## III
## Charles Igglesden - 1900

# EBONY.

FOLLOWING the road which juts out to the left as we reach the top of Appledore street we come to Ebony, a hamlet which is attached to Appledore for ecclesiastical purposes. Strange to say three churches have stood on the same spot—a very old one burnt down in Queen Elizabeth's time, its successor, which was demolished in 1858, and the present one built in that year. It was during a fearful storm in the beginning of Elizabeth's reign that the original church was struck by lightning. Flames quickly broke out, and as no fire-extinguishing appliances existed in those days the building was soon a heap of ruins, no part of it escaping destruction. Upon the foundations, however, a smaller church—or chapel, as it was called, being an appendage to Appledore—was erected. Everyone agrees in describing it as a miserable-looking building, containing one small aisle, the only attempt at architectural embellishment being a low pointed turret at the west end. No regret was expressed when in the autumn of 1858 it was demolished, for the simple reason that it stood in an inaccessible position and because the fabric was in a state of rapid decay. Its inaccessibility can the better be imagined when it is stated that the nearest building was three-quarters-of-a-mile away and that there was no path leading to it. As far as possible the material of the old church was used in the erection of the present one, which was consecrated by Archbishop Sumner in 1858 and cost only £270. The original churchyard at Ebony is still used for burials, but so small is the parish and death so uncommon amongst its inhabitants that a funeral procession is scarcely ever seen to wend its way thither. Many believe that Priory Farm at Ebony derives its title from the existence of a priory at the spot, but the truth is that the places on the oldest maps are called Priors Barn and Priors Farm because they came under the personal inspection of the Prior of Canterbury when he went on his round collecting rents. There were remains of fourteenth century work in the old barn, which was pulled down some few years ago. It is recorded that the Priors were in the habit of living at Court Lodge, Appledore, during their sojourn in the district. In those days the name of the hamlet was spelt Ebeney.

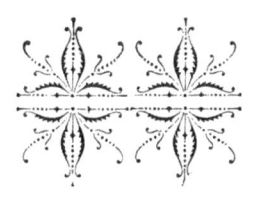

*Author's note:*
*This short essay is reproduced from Igglesden's visit in* **1900**.
*What follows, Stone-in-Oxney and Wittersham, was written in* **1923**.

AT THE FERRY STONE

Roman Altar in Vicarage Garden

THE PENANCE STONE

ANCIENT HOUSE NEAR THE CHURCH

X. Willis

## IV
## Charles Igglesden - 1923

# STONE-IN-OXNEY

THE Isle of Oxney is one of those spots in Kent where conditions have altered with the changing of rivers in their courses. A strip of land some five miles long and four miles broad it is still an island, though instead of the sea and a wide river only a narrow ditch now encircles it. On one side the river Rother and the Kent Ditch—the latter the boundary line of Kent and Sussex—run almost parallel, and a third piece of water near by and of comparatively recent construction is the Military Canal. Years ago there was much contention about this old Kent Ditch, not only here but away towards Hawkhurst, and much discussion, many conferences and even less peaceful disputes arose over the line of demarcation between the sister counties. Here at Oxney the inhabitants took the law into their own hands and deliberately severed their connection with Sussex—to which county they originally belonged—and threw in their lot with Kent. From patriotic, sentimental motives? Not at all. Merely because they realised that men of Kent possessed certain privileges not enjoyed by Sussex men. But when they had decided to become Kentish folk they found it was necessary to go through the formality of petitioning the Government to meet their wishes. They anticipated much opposition, but Sussex appeared quite pleased to lose the Islanders, perhaps to the disappointment of the latter—for no one cares to be cast away by old friends—and Oxney became a part of Kent.

It is frequently stated that the river Rother is the south boundary of the parish of Wittersham, but the Kent Ditch which runs parallel to the Rother and nearly a quarter of a mile to the north of it is the actual boundary at that point. The south-western boundary of Wittersham is the Otter Channel, which runs from the junction of the river and the Ditch at a point nearly due south of Wittersham church, north-west to Maytham Wharf and to this junction of the Rother near Blackwall Bridge. The north boundary of the Isle of Oxney

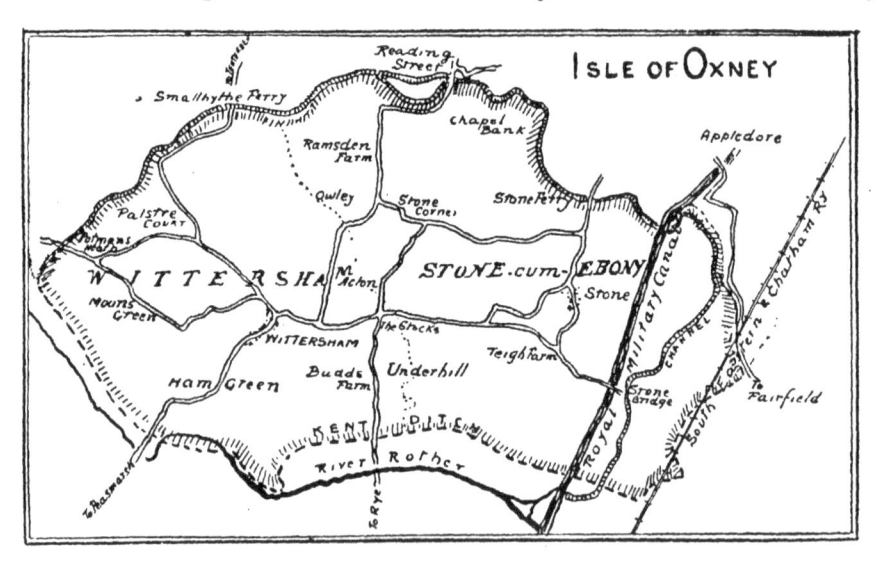

is the Reading Sewer, which runs from Potman's Heath past Smallhythe and Reading Street and joins the Canal south of Court Lodge, Appledore. Stone and Smallhythe ferries both cross the Reading Sewer, the former between Appledore and Stone, and the latter on the main road between Tenterden and Wittersham. It is interesting to know that the derivation of the word Rother is of Celtic origin and means Red Water.

In the Island itself there are two villages—Wittersham and Stone—the former being much the larger owing to its having become a residential spot for those who revel in the peacefulness of pastoral life. The administration of local government for the district has been varied at different times, and now-a-days the whole of the Isle of Oxney comes into the petty

## STONE-IN-OXNEY

sessional division of Ashford, but under the Tenterden Rural District Council and county court district. In 1894 the rural part of Ebony was added to Stone and the parish is now called "Stone-cum-Ebony."

Although the surrounding waters are very narrow you can only get into the Isle of Oxney by means of bridges and at two of them—Smallhythe and Stone—are toll-gates which shut out the traveller unless he pays a substantial amount for admittance. Other roads lead into the island where toll is not demanded. It should be remembered that at one time the sea came up as far as Smallhythe. Ferry boats plied between the mainland and the island, but it is questionable whether the crossing was made from the exact spots now occupied by the two toll-gates.

In my description of Smallhythe I have described the ferry which enters at that spot and here, close to Stone, is a similar toll-gate, with the addition of a hostelry close by, known as the Ferry Inn, and at one time the figure of a bulky ox was painted on the signboard. The good woman who now gathers in the toll is also landlady of the Inn, but the gate has been acquired by a small syndicate and brings in considerable revenue. These tolls handicap the inhabitants in every way—by making a continuous drain upon their pockets as they travel in and out although at a reduced rate, and by keeping visitors away. For now-a-days the motorist hesitates before entering a place at the price of a shilling when he can travel elsewhere for nothing. A square red-brick house by the side of the Ferry Inn was at one time the toll collector's residence. It is interesting to note the charges, which include the return journey. For four-wheeled vehicles you have to pay 1s., for two-wheeled vehicles 6d., for a bicycle 1d., a traction engine 1s. 6d., truck attached 1s., motor coach 1s. 6d., motor car 1s., motor car (two-seater) 6d., motor cycle 2d., horse, mule or ass 1d., cattle 1d., pig 1d., twenty sheep 3d., foot passenger $\frac{1}{2}$d. At night, however, it is not worth while to keep the gates closed as the traffic is slack, and should you be desirous of going in or coming out of the Isle of Oxney after ten o'clock you can do so without payment. Until quite recently the gate stood in the centre of the bridge.

A winding road takes you towards a cluster of houses some few yards ahead and here you find the white weather-boarded post office and general shop, the Crown Inn and a few modest dwellings that constitute the hamlet. A sharp rise takes you up to the ridge that runs through the Island and makes it a land-mark from the miles and miles of flat country that extends away towards the sea, with Lympne hill to your left and Rye and Winchelsea to your right. It is not a level ridge in the form of a plateau, but delightfully undulating and these few miles of Isle of Oxney soil are in rich cultivation—green pastures speckled with white-fleeced sheep, and the wheat, oats and beans all varying in tint as they start in the Spring with the faintest green and ripen out into the mellow amber tints of harvest time. Below, the water of the Royal Military Canal glistens through the boughs of the trees that line it.

A LONELY GRAVEYARD
CHAPEL MOUND

Away on your right rises a large pastured mound, bare save for a group of trees perched on its summit. Chapel Bank is its name and it lies between Stone and Reading Street. Years ago it was the site of a chapel-of-ease, but in 1858 the building was pulled down and reconstructed, from the same material, in Reading Street. It is a weird spot, up here on the summit of this mount, reached only after a tramp of a mile from the main road and then over ditches and through gates that lead into the various bits of pasture. I roamed up to the top one November afternoon and found a collection of gravestones standing about in odd places, with no suggestion of symmetry.

A hollow had been left where the foundations of the old chapel had been dug out and a couple of fir trees, with a maple and a weeping willow, now grow out of this hollow. Two sycamores stand on the outskirts of the burial ground, which is ringed by a fence. Most of the tombstones are hoary with age and moss covered, but two of them, bending downwards towards Mother Earth, had by this means secured protection from sun and rain and their inscriptions were quite legible. On others one could just decipher the names and dates, and the surfaces of others were moss-eaten and minus lettering, while more recent graves were railed in. I saw one newly made grave, with wreaths of chrysanthemums still lying upon it. For even at the present time burials take place in this strangely secluded spot. The oldest date I could find in the stones was 1699, and there were others dated 1791, 1800 and so on. Such well-known local names as Cloake, Hope, Walker, Butler, Weller, Paine and Catt were engraven upon the old stones. The fence around the burial ground is kept in repair by the incumbent of Appledore, who looks after the care of the souls at Ebony or Reading Street. It must be a strange sight to see a funeral procession winding its way from the hamlet of Reading Street, along the pastures, over tiny bridges and through primitive gates, the horses toiling up the slopes and the followers picking their way through the rough.

Down in the little hamlet of Reading Street or Ebony stands the old chapel, surrounded by a few cottages, the modern hostelry known as the White Hart and Lamb, a large building that has been at various periods a residence, the homes of four cottagers and a workhouse, and a picturesque half-timbered dwelling now belonging to Madame Jean Sterling McKinlay, of folk-song fame.

We have wandered away from Stone to explore that remarkable old site of the chapel-of-ease and the rustic little spot to which the building was removed. But the stroll was quite worth taking. We come back again to the slope upon which stands the parish church of St. Mary and revel in the glorious view from the churchyard. You are standing not quite on the crest of the hill. Looking towards the south and west a rising bit of pasture and a hill of chestnuts obscure a distant view, but, turning to the

c

north, you see the little hamlet of Stone all a cluster at the very fringe of the marshes—the inevitable cowl of an oasthouse, the bright red buildings and tiled roofs that belong to the new school of architecture under the Housing Scheme, and really old picturesque dwellings all mixed up with an air of delightful carelessness. All the country beyond is thickly studded with trees and intersected by hedgerows, while far away are the Downs known as the backbone of Kent. To the east lies the level Marsh, also profusely wooded—and only from such a point as this do you realise how much timber is grown in the Marsh—and the rows of trees that line the Military Canal form a prominent foreground. Near by are the village schools, and before they were built the youngsters were taught in the north chapel of the church. All this description gives but a faint idea of the expansive view from the churchyard, which embraces fourteen churches, while on a clear day ships can be seen in the Channel and the breakers on the shore near Lydd.

The church of St. Mary is a noble structure depicting late Perpendicular style of architecture. The material used in its construction is a mixture of hard coarse mortar—something substantial to resist the strong winds and beating rain that hurl themselves across the surrounding marshes. There is similar mortar at Davington Priory. The tower, with embattled parapet and a stair turret at one corner, is very fine and imposing, supported by well-proportioned buttresses. The hands of the restorer were set to work in 1874, and the several roofs now keep out the rain, although we are told that some eighty years ago the birds came in and brightened up the service by their chirruping and when it rained pools would collect in the aisle. All the roofs are tiled and on the eastern gable is an iron cross. Several windows have been restored, but the larger window over the west door remains weather beaten, although the smaller ones of the tower are trim with restoration. The plain west doorway, too, has been left in its dilapidated state, with battered label and the general appearance of martyrdom that accompanies age. This porch, which originally had a hipped roof that was replaced by a gabled front, is large and thick of wall, two windows being deeply splayed. The roof is carried by a tie-beam and king-post.

# STONE-IN-OXNEY

The interior has a peaceful yet bright effect from the pale blue tint of the walls, while the rays of a similar colour pour down the chancel from the glass of the east window. Looking upwards we see massive, fluted tie-beams and king-posts supporting the roof of the nave, while slighter beams cross the roof of the south chapel, which is the oldest part of the church. An elaborate king-post supports the timbered roof of the chancel, which has been recently restored with new woodwork. Unfortunately, the general view of the nave is spoilt by an ugly chimney that rises from a stove in the centre of the nave—truly a case where beauty is sacrificed for comfort.

The capacious nave has on either side a colonnade of three wide arches rising from light octagonal piers. The arches between the chancel are wide. The appearance of the several arches, since renovation, is unique and distinctly picturesque, for the architect wisely left to view the jagged edges of the stonework—an example that might have been followed by many a restorer too fond of hiding original work. Equally noticeable is the uneven, pointed archway leading to the tower, and here, as elsewhere, you have evidence of the fire with which the church was smitten.

In the south chapel are the stone steps which led to the rood loft. Above the chancel arch, which has wide chamfers, and springs from plain massive octagonal piers, are pointed windows that looked out over the chancel roof before the latter was raised during recent restoration. Another feature to notice is a projecting bowl in the south chapel. It is supposed to be a piscina, although there is no pipe by which the water could drain away. Under the arch leading from the chancel to the north chapel is a bit of the old rood screen. Perpendicular in style, the open panels contain tracery in the upper part. while more pieces of the screen partition off the north aisle from that part of the church which has been converted into a vestry. Beneath the tower arch is a screen, with ballusters. On the crossbeam are the initials of two churchwardens—W.P. and I.S.—with the date 1705. In the beam over the chancel arch is a hole through which the bell rope passed when a bell hung over the chancel.

At one time there was a craze for galleries in churches, and in the year 1721 one was erected at Stone. It disappeared a hundred years later. Other great improvements were made when the church was restored and reseated in 1874. Before leaving the church a large stone just inside the south door should be noticed, as it is of peculiar interest to antiquaries. According to tradition it is a stone upon which persons stood while doing penance, but as the position occupied by such delinquents was usually the centre of the nave, it is probable that the stone was either a stoup or the pedestal of a poor box which Edward the Third ordered to be placed in every church during his reign.

All the windows are Perpendicular and show signs of the restoration which took place about forty years ago. There is some old stained glass in the upper part of the two-light window in the north chapel and a robed figure is distinctly visible, but the rest is a hopeless jumble, bits of glass being fixed in a haphazard way. It is all of the same period and of delicate colouring. Behind the organ in the south chapel is a stained glass window erected to the memory of Anna May Inkersole, who died in 1862, aged twenty-five. The oak pulpit was erected in 1913 by his sister to the memory of Thomas Inkersole, who died in 1909. The old pulpit was pulled down and its base stands in the churchyard.

In the vestry is a mural tablet to the memory of John Cooper and his two wives, Anne and Hannah. One died in 1771 and the other in 1791, while he passed away in 1800. In the north wall is a brass tablet erected to the memory of those who lost their lives during the Great War. They are Harry Pellett, Charles E. Daw, Alfred Daw, Leonard W. Smith, Frederick B. Gill, and George Underdown, Wilfred Wenham and George Bates (who died in training). There are a few slabs on the floor of the church in which are inscriptions showing that beneath lie the mortal remains of Stephen Tighe, dated 1733; George Carter, of Kennington, and his wife, 1782 and 1765 respectively; an infant son of the Carters; John Waters, 1838; and the wife of John Hall, 1677.

While standing on the floor of the tower we are much below the surface of the churchyard ground. Above in the belfry are six bells. With the exception of the third all the bells bear the names of their makers, W. and T. Mears, William Mears and Thomas Mears, and the dates are 1786, 1787 (2), 1788 and 1795. The churchwardens, whose names are on the bells, were four in number—Sion Rofe, John Milsted, Sion Row and Stephen Samson. The third bell is supposed to have been made by I. Danyell, who lived in the middle of the fifteenth century, and belong to a series known as "Royal Arms" bells. There were similar ones at Fairfield, St. Mary's and Burmarsh. It bears the inscription VOX AGUSTINI SONET IN AURE DEI, and one of the stamps upon it represents the royal arms.

The church plate dates from the first half of the 18th century, but a rather battered pewter plate is perhaps older. The chalice weighs eight ounces and the flagon 2lbs. 6ozs. (avoirdupois). Many years ago the church possessed the heaviest chalice in Kent, but it was stolen.

One of the rectors of Stone, Thomas Spratt, eventually became Archdeacon of Rochester and was buried in Westminster Abbey in 1720. He was a fluent speaker. A more famous man connected with Stone was Sir Thomas Wyatt, who at one time owned land in the parish but exchanged it for property at Boxley. At the time of his unsuccessful revolution he was supported by a number of men from the Isle of Oxney, but what fate befel them is not recorded.

In the year 1552 an inventory of all parish church goods was officially made in Kent and the following is the Stone list :—

> William Goche, curate, Johh Dobynson, gent. churchwarden.
> First on chalice with the patente of silver parcel gilt weighing xii ounces.
> Item one holy water stokke of latten.
> Item on paire of sensers of latten.
> Item iij bells in the steple suted of brasse a saints bell of brasse & two sacrying bells of brass.
> Item a cross of coppe and on herse crosse.
> Item on vestmente of red damaske with the deacon of the same sute of the gifte of Sir John Wilshire knyghte.

25

Item on other vestmente of white damaske with a ctosse of velvett.
Item a vestment of olf red silk with lyons upon it with deacon & subdeacon to the same of the same sute.
Item a canapie of red satten with the V wounds upon the cape thereof.
Item on herse clothe of blacke silke with a crosse of lynnen cloth.
Item llj tynnacles one of white and blewe dorynx, the second of grene saie with a blew cross the third of grene silk ahd threde the gifte of John Franke.
Item a corprax case of red and blew velvett and one other corprax case of yellowe and black velvett.
Item on corprax case of red velvett imbrothered with gold & one other corprax case of white silke.
Item on corprax case of grene dornyx.
Item iij chists to laye old things in & on chiste for the register booke.

In the year 1573 Archbishop Parker sent round a commission to enquire into the state of the various parishes in East Kent. The result was a report which showed that the average instance in which the parson was non-resident was one in six. At Stone it was reputed that the Vicar had not read the "Quenes Mats Iniunctions this twelve-month," and that "they have lacked theire quarter sermons this twelve month in the defaulte of theire vicar." The church was reported to have "the chauncell in decay," a Lovelace being responsible for its repair. The entire church "lacketh reparations and the churche yarde walles." John Potte and Robert Water were reported backward in the payment of scottes, and finally a village scandal arose because Thomas Lydden and Joan Judge after being thrice asked in church "do not procede to the solemmizacon of matrimony, but kepe together in howse suspiciously, to the offence of the congregacon."

The vicarage stands nearly opposite the church—a modern house—and in the front garden is an ancient stone Roman altar, which was removed from the church. On each side is rudely carved the figure of an ox. At the top is a bowl and near the base an iron ring, to which it is suggested the animal to be sacrificed was bound. After its removal from the church it was used as a horse block and greatly mutilated, but in 1777 the Vicar of the day had it restored and placed in its present position.

At the side of the churchyard is a quaint old half-timbered building, its oak framework filled in with plaster. In the front are two over-hangs supported by massive corner-posts. Between these over-hangs is a remarkable little dormer window, jutting forward and perched on a massive bracket.

There is one charity in Stone, Richard Still in 1556 leaving a sum of money which brings in 13s. 4d. a year, and is distributed among the aged poor of the parish.

The Baptist Chapel stands between the ferry gate and the parish church—a building with no artistic merit, constructed of painted timber with tiled roof. It is attached to an old cottage, and there is a small graveyard outside. Within is a baptistry and the seating accommodates about sixty persons. There is no resident minister, the services being conducted by a circuit preacher from Tenterden or Romney Marsh. The chapel is of considerable age, probably having been built over a hundred and fifty years ago, but there appear to be no documents showing the exact date of its erection.

# V
## Charles Igglesden - 1923

# WITTERSHAM

THE peculiar fascination about this spit of Kent known as the Isle of Oxney extends to its remotest corners. It is a place where imagination can be let loose, where out of the peaceful pastures of to-day rise visions of deadly combat, when invaders from Scandinavia—piratical Vikings and the like—came in their ships, landed and butchered the astonished islanders. The tide of the Channel flowed around the bit of undulating land and we can well conceive how, shut off from the mainland, the rustic inhabitants lived a life of complacent ease, self-contented as isolated people become in time, jealous of the "foreigner" who lived across the narrow channel. They would inter-marry and deteriorate in stamina; indeed, there was an old saying that "the Marshman died of ague, the Oxney Islander of madness." They must have degenerated like the Dutch of Walcheren and other parts of Holland, upon whose islands families still intermarry and present a sorry spectacle of idiotic inanity.

But the last two centuries have wrought a change, and with the silting of the land and the receding of the sea the old island is now practically merged into the neighbouring part of Kent. Smuggling went on with reckless daring, the levels below forming easy landing places, while the hillocks of the island itself formed natural "hides," and not one of those old timbered houses that so innocently dot the countryside to-day can plead

THE CHURCH

QUAINT CORBELS AT WITTERSHAM CHURCH

REMAINS OF MOAT PALSTRE COURT

THE STOCKS

# WITTERSHAM

guiltless of being the haunt of smuggler or receiver. Then, as to-day, the land was kept in rich cultivation, producing its wealth of hops and corn and pastures upon which cattle and sheep fattened, the cattle especially finding fit food for healthy appetite in the levels through which the ditches even now run and overflow in winter time until the Rother Valley looks like a shimmering lagoon.

Yes, truly fascinating is this bit of land that marks the extreme boundary of Kent as she joins up with Sussex. If you cross Stone Ferry you must go ahead; there is no turning back. Winding roads crawling up the little slope are too tempting. You long to know what is beyond these hills, and a placid stillness reigns everywhere as you wend your way to Wittersham. So still is it at times that you can hear the munching of cattle or sheep as they tear off the rich blades of grass. Then, when a breeze springs up, there is the faint rustle of the trees, or maybe, high overhead, the encouraging song of the lark to his mate as she sits patiently in her nest below, while he imagines himself equally busy chortling and flapping his tiny wings aloft. Grassy swards, some wide, some narrow, skirt the roadway, and here in summer time myriad butterflies draw honey from the wild flowers. Indeed, the Isle of Oxney was once known as a haunt of rare insects, but an entymologist tells me that there is no longer any distinctive feature among the moths and butterflies of this part of Kent.

Having passed Stone Ferry you soon come to two turnings, one of which takes you up the hill to Stone and the other winds away towards Wittersham. Following the more direct road you pass through the former village and then along a roadway, with wide bordering of grass reaching away to the quickset hedges. You steadily climb a hill, and on the left see substantial dull-bricked homesteads, dotted here and there, but nothing modern. Even brick and tile are tinted with the soft shades of age.

But you can walk from the Ferry along a road that winds round away from the village of Stone and takes you up to the cross-roads known as the Stocks. Immediately you leave the Ferry you revel in the twisting lanes. At one spot hops grow prolifically and on a rise in the ground are two oasthouses, standing like two dignified sentinels keeping watch over the green grapelike branches as they turn from pale green to rich yellow, when they will be engulfed within the walls of these same round oasts and crushed and dried for the making of beer. On the other side, on the day I sauntered along through the winding lanes, were sheaves of richest coloured wheat which no rain had tarnished, the hedges were dotted with wild nuts and deep purple blackberries, and some distance beyond rose that smooth mound known as Chapel Bank—a closely nibbled piece of pasture relieved only by a few trees perched prominently on the summit, which, by the by, can be seen for many miles around, and are said to have been the favourite look-out of the smugglers and a landmark for sailormen.

Further along is a house indisputably old, carrying us back to the timber age. The modern brick front hides the old framework and matchboarding surmounts the overhanging storey of one wing. The original site of the old wing remains unsullied by modern work and you can see the weather-worn timber, with plaster filling in the square panels. Here again is a very long overhang supported by tiny brackets instead of the huge corner posts that you find in other parts of Kent. Two little windows are perched up under the eaves, showing that the old builders were not only economical in the lighting of their rooms but that when they had the chance they placed their windows—strange freak!—where the sun's rays could only penetrate with difficulty. The low pitch of the rooms had much to do with this arrangement.

Just past the turning that leads to Ebony you find another timbered house of less importance than the other farmsteads in the island, but its thatched roof gives it a touch of the picturesque that the others do not possess. You are all this time climbing a hill, and reaching its summit find yourself entering the village. On one side are oast houses. Just past a white wind-mill, and half hidden by huge chestnut trees is a tumble-down looking building which looks as if it had weathered the storms of many centuries and almost collapsed at its last gasp. The roof is undulating in sympathy with the shrunken rafters within. The outer plaster is allowed to remain grimy and grey and the timbers that form the framework, and even the old Tudor door with its iron studs, have not seen a coat of paint for many a day. Truly a revelation of what can be done in the restoration of an old Tudor house. For it has been renovated, this quaint old place called The Stocks, but with artistic care. A few years ago it was but a tumble-down shadow of its former glory—for it must have been a pretentious building and the property of pretentious people—but Mr. Norman Forbes-Robertson saw great possibilities in its restoration and purchased it. Retaining all the original framework and obtaining old timber for renewals he reproduced it in the style that it originally presented. And the result is delightful. The old windmill comes into The Stocks domains, and, no longer turning to the wind and grinding corn, like so many other war-worn veterans no longer wanted, it has become a summer-house.

The obvious conclusion is that the village stocks stood at this spot, and the only reason for thinking otherwise is that they were usually placed nearer the heart of a village not far from the church. We read of a whipping post at Wittersham, and it is recorded that a woman named Goody Burden suffered this painful and ignominious punishment. The law for whipping women was repealed in 1820, so Goody Burden must have fallen into trouble previous to that date. Women were whipped for immorality, and possibly Goody Burden was an unfortunate. There were, however, other sins considered heinous enough to deserve this form of punishment. For instance, two women were whipped at Ashford because they had smallpox, and the sum of eightpence was paid to the man for chastising them. This was in the days when lunatics were treated in the same way and then chained up to a wall like a dog. Good old days!

A little further along is another old oast house—what a lot of hops they must have grown hereabouts if so many oasthouses were required—and this one is converted into a room with a strange little tiled cap taking the place of the old cowl. Adjoining is a tiny building once a barn. This is now the combined studio and quiet study of Mrs. Long, who, writing under the nom-de-plume of Marjorie Bowen, became a novelist as a girl and created a storm of enthusiasm in literary circles by her historical novel, "The Viper of Milan," and is the leading woman novelist of to-day.

Still higher we go and the fresh breeze fans our faces, fresh and exhilarating with a touch of salt from the sea not far away. On one side high wooded hills, on the other the Sussex coast and the yellow sand dunes of Camber stretching away towards the sea. Shipping? Yes, ships are in sight, their white sails glimmering as specks in the sunlight; large liners and lesser craft that care not which way the wind may blow leave trails of lazy smoke to hover over the rippling blue. Turn again and there is Tenterden church, with its historical steeple standing prominently on the ridge where the town is built, and down in the hollows, from Rye away to Tenterden, is the Rother Valley. The Kent Ditch, that stagnant bit of water that divides Kent from Sussex, runs almost parallel with the River Rother.

Still strolling along we reach a corner where stands a large house—converted cottages—the whole transformation carried out in so skilful a way that a few years hence it will deceive the eye and pass muster as a seventeenth century house. On this site stood Hurst, an ancient house that disappeared many years ago — it is believed a victim to fire — but the cottages now converted were erected in its place.

Yet a second wind-mill and even another oast-house are to be found as you get nearer the church, and at the corner is a hostelry known as the Ewe and Lamb, a classic building if we are to judge by the two little columns of Grecian character supporting the front, each surmounted by a medallion. Across the road is a house some two hundred years old, or even more, with that same type of hipped roof which I have already mentioned as popular in Kent architecture since the coming of the Flemish weavers, and mathematical tiles. That little butcher's shop jutting out at the corner gives the spot a picturesque touch.

Across the way, on a conspicuous site, stands the War Memorial, of singularly beautiful design, on which the names of Wittersham's dead heroes are inscribed:—H. C. Bathup, Lincs. Regt.; S. C. Dengate, R. Irish Regt.; H. T. Slingsby, The Buffs; R. T. Carter, M.C., R.G.A.; G. J. Nash, R.A.S.C.; L. L. Collings, R.F.A.; T. C. Ashdown, R. Sussex Regt.; J. F. Wilkinson, M.C., R.F.A.; F. Hinkley, Sherwood Foresters; G. G. Wilson, L.N. Lancs. Regt.; T. J. Phillpotts, Middlesex

# WITTERSHAM

Regt.; S. Knight, R. Fusiliers; A. W. Turner, R.F.A.; T. A. Wollett, The Buffs; J. G. Russell, The Buffs; H. V. Hoad, The Buffs; E. E. Woollett, The Buffs; W. Maynard, The Buffs; J. Ades, The Buffs; A. H. Catt, The Buffs; W. H. Addy, R.G.A.; A. Paine, The Buffs. At the side are the words "Lest We Forget" and "To those who died for us."

Near here is a quaint old-world building, a projecting shop running out from a house some three hundred years of age. Weather-boarding covers the timbers in one instance, while tiles hang in front of the adjoining building with its long roof sweeping down to within a few feet of the ground. Its trimness might leave you to think that brick and tile constituted the

*Neves Shop*

structure, but inside you find the tell-tale beams—those heavy baulks of the famous Weald—that carry us back into the long ago. Besides the oak beams open hearths remain. For several generations it has been known as "Neve's Shop," and for the very good reason that until comparatively recent days it was the only shop in Wittersham and the name of Neve has always been connected with it. The founder of the Neve family was John le Neve, a Hugenot of the Provencal family of "Le Noveau," and he left France shortly after the massacre of St. Bartholomew and landed at Rye on September 10th, 1572. His descendants have resided at Wittersham and Sandhurst since then, and the business then started in the former place has been in the same family for upwards of three centuries. During the last century it has only changed hands twice. The present owner's grandfather, David Neve, was here in 1800; his son, Thomas Rootes Neve, came into possession in 1850, and Benjamin Amos Neve has been installed in the home of his ancestors since 1900. His grandfather was wont to make two journeys per annum to London to buy stock for the six months, riding up on horse-back and taking two days on the way. The goods came down to Wittersham two or three weeks later by waggon, often arriving at midnight. At that time, and even within the last sixty years, a large part of the goods came by sea to Rye in coasting vessels from Holland, France and the north of England.

What a delightful picture of these happenings can be recalled in imagination? And then, aroused from reverie, we look along the old road and crash goes all thought of romance. For the modern builder has come into his own and there stands his handicraft in the array of red-brick houses which the housing problems of to-day demand. Necessary, but—! Another change in the aspect of the village has been caused by the destruction of the grand old windmill that stood across a meadow just off the roadway. It was a distinctive mark for miles around.

Around the church is a cluster of many buildings, old and new, but mainly old enough to wear the mellow tints that make of them a snug and happy little family picture. The space that was once an open Green has been built over, and judging from the age of some of the buildings the usurpation of the common rights of the village commenced over a hundred years ago. Six hundred years since, when fairs could only be held by consent of King or Queen, Wittersham was granted permission to hold one annually on May 1st. The stalls were filled with toys and pedlars had their pitch and sold many and varied articles on this old Green. Here now stands the village hall. By the side of the church and shadowed by yet another oast-house is the elementary school, and a tablet near tells us that to commemorate the coronation of the present King water was laid on to the village.

Adjoining the churchyard which, by-the-by, is sheltered by stalwart limes and spreading chestnuts, is a jumbled mass of buildings whose roofs of many shapes run into each other, showing that at one time they belonged to one owner. They are the roofs of the Queen's Head and its stables with houses adjoining.

Northward of the church is a large red-brick house which stands on the site of the ancient manor house or court lodge. In the reign of Richard the Second it was given to the College of All Saints, Maidstone, and we read that subsequently Henry the Fourth made the property more secure by granting a formal license to the Masters and Fellows of that College to hold the "manor of Wyghtresham and its appurtenances." Then came the blow from Henry the Eighth—that decree which suppressed this and all similar colleges. Wittersham College was its name at the time, and among the many owners were the Crispes, Sir Thomas Bishop and William Blackmore, of Tenterden, and now it is the property of Colonel John Body, who is lord of the manor. For centuries the place went by the name of Wittersham College, but a few years ago it became known as Wittersham Court.

Beyond the schools is a house now belonging to Mrs. John Body, its front a mass of ivy and ampelopsis. Within is a delightful chimney corner with a superb old fire back, embossed with the figure of an armour-clad knight mounted on a charger. Just across the way is an old-world house with virginia creeper entwining its tendrils among the tiles — tiles, beware ! — and meandering over its roof, while close by is another house recently enlarged but wearing the garb of the distinct style of architecture that predominates in Wittersham. You find much timber inside these buildings, denoting that the framework was of wood, but bricks and tiles encase it nowadays. The hipped roof prevails, a style that bluntly finishes off the side of a house, reminding one of the stern of the old Spanish galleons. In one of the houses opposite Wittersham church lives a daughter of the late

Alma Tadema, the eminent artist. And this reminds me of the interesting coterie that has gathered together here in this little village perched upon the ridge of Oxney Isle. I have already mentioned names to conjure with—Marjorie Bowen for literature, Norman Forbes-Robertson for the drama, Alma Tadema for art, and in addition there is the name of Lyttleton—famous in sport and politics. The Hon. Alfred Lyttleton lived at the old Vicarage, and Mrs. Lyttleton still resides there. "Birds of a feather flock together," and a short time since Robert Hichens, the novelist, was living at Wittersham.

The church stands in the centre of the village street and at a strange angle with the road-way and churchyard wall. You enter by a lych-gate and face one of the most beautiful towers in this part of Kent. You have to gaze upwards, very far upwards ere you focus its buttresses and its windows, let alone the embattled summit. The buttresses are tall and elegantly proportioned. The whole tower is equally symmetrical and all the windows are large and imposing, while a narrow turret, running up at one corner, is ornamented with an embattled parapet. So lofty is the tower that the pointed roof of the nave and the flat roof of the north aisle seem dwarfed by comparison. A truly typical Perpendicular window is over the west doorway, while the latter, although battered, still gives evidence of the fine workmanship of the fourteenth century. The arch of the doorway rises from slender columns, while the spandrells are panelled. The label is supported by what were once angels bearing shields, but one figure has entirely disappeared and the outline of the other is only just discernable.

But why the disfiguration at the corner of the church? Why that unsightly little shed placed between the buttresses of the tower? That water tank, too! And again, that chimney! All this is a cruel wrong to those fifteenth century masons who raised with loving care and artistic taste that fine old tower of Wittersham church.

The exterior of the south aisle bears evidence of extensive restoration and one window has been left severely alone—possibly to be held up as an awful example of the power of the elements and what inroads they can make upon stone mullions left in their helplessness. And yet there is something grand in

# WITTERSHAM

the grey weather-beaten stone walls of an old church that may have suffered greatly from the elements and can still stand with grim erectness to show they have never entirely succumbed to the ravages of wind, frost and rain.

Here at Wittersham the church shows traces of conflict in the dull green-grey tint of stone that once was white: some of it is mellowed with yellow or amber moss, and even tufts of green weed jut out of the mortar between the stones. Over the restored east window of the south aisle two corbel heads have been preserved, the faces being those of a king and queen. Other corbels, more modern, are to be seen in the east window of the chancel. The restorer of the church not many years ago must have revelled in the love of corbels, for he has even placed two in the little doorway that leads to the vestry.

The interior of the church of St. John the Baptist discloses work of various periods of architecture. The oldest part is Early English of the twelfth century, then follows the Decorated style and finally Perpendicular. The spaciousness of the building gives an air of brightness, yet the almost glaring light of the large white western window is subdued as we near the altar by the dark blue and deep crimson colouring of the stained-glass window in the east. The flags of the Allies of the Great War are suspended over the chancel, which was rebuilt in 1892. The pitch of the nave is high and the roof supported by tie beams from which spring king-posts conspicuous for their elegant moulding. The roof of the south aisle has slighter tie beams with king-posts, but the roof of the north aisle is almost flat, crossed by unplaned beams. As I have said, the windows are almost entirely plain, but there are little bits of old coloured glass in the north aisle. In the chancel is a small stained-glass window erected to the Rev. E. R. Nares and his wife Mary. He was rector and died in 1865, while his wife died the following year. The large east window above the altar is peculiarly rich in colouring—deep crimson and blue. There is, in addition, an artistic bit of stained-glass work in the west window of the north aisle, quite different in style to the formal designs usually connected with coloured glass in churches. It represents St. Augustine landing in England in 597, while two angels herald his approach. School children collected funds for its purchase.

D

Some old stained-glass windows have disappeared, for the historian Harris tells us that two hundred years ago, in the east window of the north chancel (called Acton Chancel), were the Arms of Watton, anciently owner of the Manor of Palstre, "and in the first of the north windows in this chancel is a memorial of the ancient family of Petlesden; and near the entrance one of Audian or Odiarne, once owner of Acton."

One of the most interesting features connected with the church is the different style of architecture to be seen in the arcades of five arches on each side of the nave. On the north side are two of Early English date rising from circular pillars with plain capitals. Two others are of the later Decorated period, octagonal, with richly moulded capitals and having concave faces. The arch at the west end of this arcade dies into the wall, while the respond of the one in the far east is an elegant Early English shaft, the capital being embellished with foliated carving. The hoods of two of these arches are supported by corbels. Crossing to the south side of the nave we find the arches rising from octagonal piers which, with the exception of one, have concave faces and, as on the north side, the outside arches die into the walls.

What attracts you inside the church, as well as outside, is the number of corbel heads or masks to be seen in many places. Some are older than others, but generally speaking are not the awful contortions of the human face that one so often sees depicted. There are six which support the hoods of the nave arches, all the faces being different, two more embellish the chancel arch, and the hoods of the two arches that lead from the chancel to the aisles are also supported by corbels in the form of human faces more grotesque than the others.

The various arches in the church are lofty, and specially impressive in this respect is the one that admits us to the tower. Its mouldings, carried on circular shafts with octagonal capitals, are bold. Beneath is a screen, on the doors of which are carved the words, "Open to me the gates of righteousness. I will go into them and I will praise the Lord." Around the ground floor of the tower are stone seats. The chancel arch has short shafts springing from the walls and supported by foliated carving of rare beauty. The two arches that lead from the

# WITTERSHAM 43

chancel to the aisles are exceptionally wide and give this part of the church an atmosphere of space. Against the screens under the arches are fixed the choir stalls. Remains of a benatura are in the wall just within the south doorway. Above the arches at the west end another old-time relic will be found in faint traces of a fresco. Beneath a window is a trefoiled piscina, the head rising above the sill. A sedilia in the chancel has three seats and close by is a piscina; each has a trefoiled head. The choir seats have richly carved ends, and in the vestry is an ancient wooden altar table with claw feet. The lectern is five hundred years old, exceptionally large and carved, the cornice being decorated with fleur-de-lys and crosses. The side is chamfered and in the trefoil is the Angus Dei. It revolves on a panelled circular stern, and at the feet are crosspieces beautifully carved. The font is modern and consists of an octagonal bowl with trefoiled arches in the sunken panels. On the floor of the north aisle are remnants of an old brass. The figure is that of a man wearing a cloak with the inscription: "Pray for the soule of Stevyn Audyan which decessed ye xxiii. day of Aprill in the yer' of our Lord God a thousand ccccc. xxiii. on whose soule Jhu have mcy Ame." This quaint inscription shows that it commemorates one of the family referred to by Harris, and is additionally interesting from the following particulars recorded in Testamenta Cantiana: "To be buried in the north side of the Church of St. John the Baptist at the end of my seat there, and my exors. to cause a stone, price 26s. 8d., to be laid over my body there," from the will of Stephen Odearn, 1523.

Memorials are scarce. On the walls of the tower hangs a framed statement that the remains of the Rev. M. Cornwallis and his wife are deposited under a stone in the centre of the chancel floor. He died in 1827 and she in 1836. He was rector for fifty years. There is also a slab in the chancel floor with the name of Harris carved upon it. Against the south wall is an elegant brightly coloured marble memorial to the Hon. Alfred Lyttleton, the well-known athlete and statesman, who settled in Wittersham towards the end of his life. He died in 1913. On the south wall is a brass recording the names of those who gave up their lives in the Great War, while on a small oak cabinet near the tower arch are inscribed the names of all Wittersham men who joined the colours.

The bells number five of various dates. Three are dated 1609. Two bear the inscription, Josephus Carter me fecit, but the third has, in addition, the following:—" Thomas Odiarne, Jeremy Odiarne, Isaake Odiarne, gave this bell, 1609." The tenor bell is inscribed " John Wilmar made me—IB—GF—CW, 1629." The newest bell is dated 1808, with the name of the well-known firm, Thomas Mears and Son, engraved on it. The task of bringing heavy bells up the hill to Wittersham, probably by oxen, must have been hard work. They were made in London and taken to Rye by sea. One word of regret—the framework and fittings inside the tower are in a poor state of repair; yet the Wittersham bells possess a most beautiful and mellow tone and should be jealously preserved.

In the report of Archbishop Parker's visitation the following complaints are made : " That theire parson is not resident and they never sawe hym, and he geveth not to the poor accordinge to the Queen's injunctions." Also that the parish presented Johane Davy, that she had committed a crime with one Willms Hogs." Further, Willms Robyus was reported " because he will not pay his scotte to the collectors for the poore."

During the reign of Charles the First the clergy of the Church of England suffered persecution, and a peculiar instance of the hounding down of an unfortunate man occurred when one Thomas Tourney, rector of Wittersham, was the victim. His house was plundered several times, and on one occasion his horse was stolen. Whether by design or accident it so happened that the theft of his horse was a serious matter, as on the following day he was compelled to go to Tenterden to meet various accusations brought against him and the only way to reach that town was by borrowing a steed. The animal turned out to be a restive young mare, and while going down the hill near Smallhythe, on his return home, his bridle broke and he was thrown " just against the Chapel-of-Ease which is in that street." This was sufficient evidence for a second charge to be preferred against him—of being drunk while riding the horse. He was promptly sent to prison. The principal witness against him was a farmer, who had sworn to turn him out of Wittersham, and it eventually became known that he had perjured himself. But he met with a ghastly death. While shooting ducks in the Marshes he came upon a patch of quick-sand, and, being alone, was unable to extricate himself. As the tide was coming in at that time the struggling victim was slowly drowned. The record of this tragedy is interesting because it shows that the tidal sea at one time came up to Smallhythe. Within a few days of the death of his arch enemy Thomas Tourney was released from prison, and with his wife and three young children took a farm at Stone, having been compelled to give up the church. But his privations left their mark upon him and he soon died, leaving his family, as an old record states, " in a very poor condition."

Wittersham boasted of two old moated manor houses, and the remains of these defences are still to be seen. You pass one of them, Owlie, on the way to Reading Street, but it stands so far back from the highway that you cannot see it unless you take a long walk. Here at the end of the farm road it stands quite alone. Tiles and bricks cover up the wooden interior, and the beams in the rooms are whitewashed. Partitions have been added and the rooms are now square. The remains of a moat can be clearly seen. Now, it should be remembered that the existence of a moat around a building did not necessarily invest it with the importance of a fortress; it merely acted as a defence against marauding bands who were in the habit of making attacks upon isolated buildings, and here, at Owlie, anciently known as Oveley, resided a wealthy family in very early days, and bearing the name of Oveley. It has been suggested to me that the family of Oveley took their name from the name of place, which possibly dated back to Anglo-Saxon times. May it not have been Owl-ey—the owl's island—ey being Teutonic for island? Enclosed within its moat the property would form an island, while the choice of name might have been strengthened by the fact that the spot itself was situated on an island—the Isle of Oxney—an island within an island. Or might not the name have been Ow-ley—ley, lei (Anglo-Saxon leigh), meaning an open space in a wood? Tenterden, close by, as "den" implies, lay in a deep, wooded valley, and Ow, the corruption of the name of some far-a-way

Jutish possessor of the land? The subject forms an interesting point in the absorbing study of place-names. During the reign of Henry the Second the family of Odiarne became possessed of it, and they continued in possession until the reign of Henry the Eighth, when it was sold to one John Maney, of Biddenden, who then sold it to Sir Peter Ricaut. Subsequently it became the property of the Knights of Godmersham. The Odiarnes appear to have been of great note in this part of the country, and their arms were at one time painted in the window of the north chancel of Wittersham Church. Coming to more recent years I find that both Owley and Palstre belonged to William Levett, who died in 1842, when Owley went to Mrs. Samuel Rutley. At his death in 1900 the property was sold.

In addition to Owley there was another large house close by known as Ascheden, which stood on the site of the house now known as Acton Chantry, and was part of the possessions of the owner of Owley. This house stands on the Reading Street road not far from Owley, and, although the front is modern, there are indications of age in other parts of the building. Inside is old timber, including handsome beams.

By far the most historic spot in Wittersham is Palstre Court. It stands in a part of the parish known as Pinyon Quarter. You reach it by strolling from the village towards Wittersham Road railway station—a house with a white front standing some little distance away from the roadside. The house is possibly three or four hundred years old, but its exterior, now brick and tiled, might deceive you as to its age. Walk inside, however, and you will see at once that the interior of the main building is of the timbered period. Oak beams support the first floor, and up in the roof are fine old rafters and more heavy beams. Below in one of the rooms is the original fireplace, a mighty oak beam running its whole length, some fourteen feet. Here, too, are chimney-corners with an old fire-plate, in front of which logs burn crisply in the winter time. The old crane from which was suspended the cauldron still stands by the side of the chimney. Such is Palstre Court to-day —a homely farmhouse—but the original residence stood several yards away on an enclosure within a moat, and fruit trees grow on its old foundations. The moat is very clearly defined and

## WITTERSHAM 47

runs practically in a square all round the ground upon which Palstre Court stood. Dig where you will on this spit of land and you will come across the old foundations of what was once the finest mansion in this part of England. There is a tradition that much buried treasure lies underground round about Palstre Court, but extensive excavations have taken place without result.

The history of Palstre goes back as far as any possession in Kent, for it is mentioned even as long ago as 1032. In an old charter of that date it is stated that King Canute gave it to Christ Church, Canterbury, "as foster-land for his soul." Foster-land was land given for the good and sustenance of the monks. When William the Conqueror parcelled out the land he gave Palstre to Odo, Bishop of Bayeaux, who, however, fell into disgrace, and the rich gifts that had been showered upon him were confiscated. So another Court favourite took possession and the new owner adopted the name of Palstre. But the reign of Edward the Third saw another change, for the Basing family bought it, together with part tolls of Smallhythe Ferry. Among subsequent owners was Sir Thomas Wyatt, who failed in his rebellion and lost his property, and more recent owners were the Levetts. The estate now belongs to the widow of Lieut.-Colonel Heyworth, who bought it some years ago, planted the orchards and restored most of the moat.

Years ago a desperate feud existed between the lads of the towns and villages that lay on the border between Kent and Sussex. At one time Rye and Wittersham were embroiled to such an extent that it was unsafe for Rye men to be in the Isle of Oxney after dark and equally risky for Wittersham men to be found even near the Rother, let alone in close proximity. The brawling arose after an amorous youth from Rye had eloped with a Wittersham wench. Furious at losing his fiancee the Wittersham swain collected his friends and, under cover of an anonymous letter, enticed the bridegroom to come to a meeting place close by the Rother. Need I describe the sequel? The Wittersham bravadoes promptly captured him and threw him into the river. It was only by a miracle that he was saved from drowning. Within a few days the bargees of Rye crossed the Rother, boldly entered the village, thrashed the disappointed lover and returned the compliment of dragging him to the river and throwing him in. But this act of revenge was not accomplished without bloodshed, for Wittersham rose to a man and attacked the Rye lads down in the marshes and, according to the London Chronicle of 1799, several heads and limbs were broken.

# VI
# Malcolm Horton Revisit - 2024

## Isle of Oxney

Igglesden visited the Isle of Oxney's three villages, Wittersham, Stone and Ebony in 1923, although he had briefly visited Ebony in 1900. This gap may be an acknowledgement that Ebony was a separate and

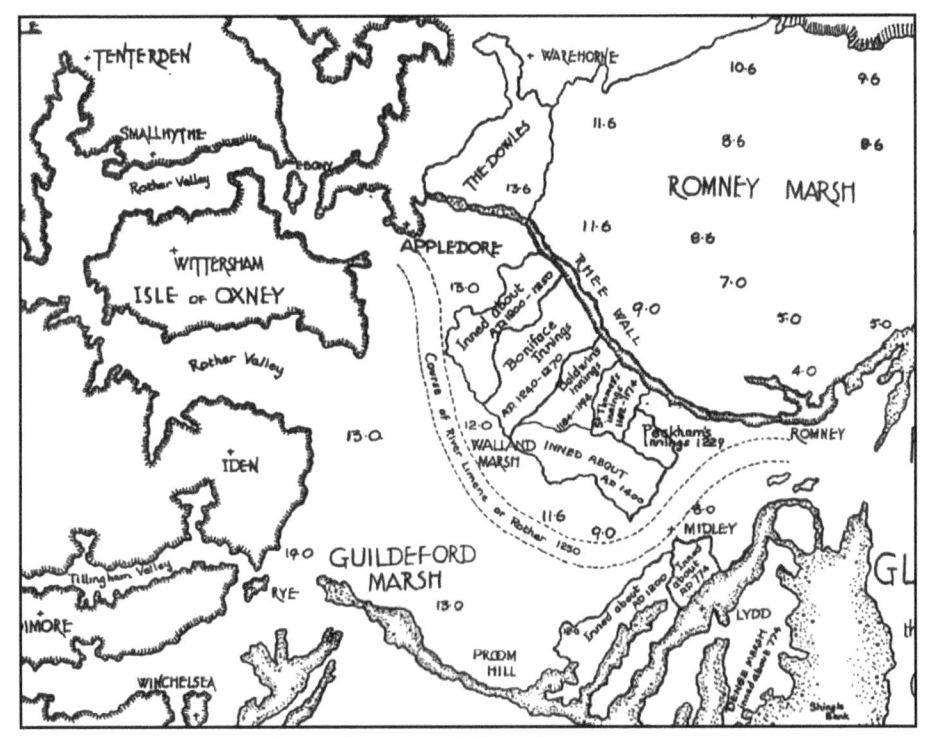

Map of Oxney and Ebony 14th century

somewhat mysterious island, which had existed for over 1,000 years, until the waterway which separated Ebony from mainland Kent and the Isle of Oxney, silted up after the 17th century.

The Island of Oxney including Ebony is quite small, measuring 5½ miles west to east and 3½ miles north to south. Its boundaries are still delineated by water but now in mere ditches on three sides, all of which were once navigable. The River Rother borders the south of the island before flowing down to Rye an offshoot connects with the Reading Sewer which becomes Potmans Heath Channel for a short section to the the west of the island before flowing round the northern side of the island and, just below Appledore, joins The Royal Military Canal, to form the eastern boundary.

The reason for this change, in such a short space of time, was explained to me by distinguished Kent Archaeologist Dr Andrew Richardson. It is due to the fact that the coast line around Oxney, and the adjoining Romney Marsh, is extremely dynamic, due to both natural causes and also the intervention of man.

Until the 14$^{th}$ century the River Rother had two channels, one flowing round the north of Oxney and the other to the south, both ending up in Rye. Both Rye and Small Hythe have been international trading

Isle of Oxney

ports going back to the days of the Phoenicians pre-Roman times, who were frequent visitors as were the Venetians and traders from Florence. The excellent Tenterden Museum contains many artefacts both pottery and coins going back to Roman times and the 13$^{th}$ century in the days of Edward I. Man intervened in 1336 and dammed up the southerly flow of the Rother (the Knelle Dam), diverting it through the North Channel which made for a deep water channel around Small Hythe and Reading Street, forcing the Rother to flow up to Tenterden. This resulted in Tenterden acquiring Cinque Port status in 1449. Important boat building locations were established at Small Hythe and Reading Street. Reading Street's main claim to fame was building Henry VII's 600 ton vessel, Regent. Incidentally it is thought that a wealthy family by the name of Small gave its name to Small Hythe

The process of ship building used was a bespoke method, involving digging a hexagonal basin in the mud immediately behind the shoreline of a size commensurate with that of the ship to be built. Once the ship was finished the boat was launched into the waterway by breeching the shoreline at high tide, and allowing it to float out into waterway. The remains of these basins can be seen in the field opposite Small Hythe Place and recent excavations have found hundreds of discarded nails and fixings from the ship-building period.

There are two pieces of folklore associated with the Isle of Oxney gleefully–repeated by Igglesden, because local folklore, traditions and superstitions were part- of the defining characteristics of his village essays.

One of these concerns its remoteness from the mainland in times gone by which led to much inter-marrying and the high incidence of insanity on the island. The other in Igglesden's Stone essay, as pointed out by Dr Andrew Richardson, is a perfect example of historians, including Igglesden, merely quoting a previous historian.

In this case the historian in question was the ubiquitous Edward Hasted in the late 18th century. He related the story passed down by previous historians that Oxney had, in the past, been part of Sussex, whose inhabitants perceived that their next door neighbours in Kent, enjoyed greater privileges, granted to them by the Normans in 1066. Wishing to avail themselves of those greater privileges the good people of Oxney petitioned to become part of Kent. In this they were successful. However as related by Andrew Richardson a Charter was discovered dated 724AD granting an uninhabited area known as Brentisleag (now Tenterden) and the Island of Oxney to St Mildred, Abbess of Minster on the Isle of Thanet, for the purpose of grazing of pigs in winter. What made this area so suitable for this purpose was the abundance of acorns from the oak trees in the Weald.

Saint Mildred

(Then known by its Saxon name of Anreasweald This Charter was granted by Aethelberht King of Kent. So it would seem that in 724AD Oxney must have already been in Kent. In relation to Tenterden a settlement grew up in Brentisleag and it gained the name Tenterden from this Charter of 724AD. It means Tenet-ware-den; a clearing in the forest (Den) for the men of Thanet. Further confirmation of the connection with Minster Abbey was the dedication of Tenterden Church to St Mildred in the late 8th century.

At this time Oxney would have been inhabited, because we know that the Romans had a settlement there until around 300AD. Roman coins up until this time have been found around Stone on what would have been the south coast of the Island of Oxney. Roman coins have not been found from a later period, indicating that the departure was somewhat sudden. According to Andrew Richardson the climate at this time suddenly became much colder.

The most famous Roman artefact found on Oxney is the Mithraic alter piece currently residing in Stones Church. Mithras was the pagan god worshipped by Roman soldiers. The Mithraic alter measures 3 feet 4 inches in height and is more or less 2 feet square. More about that later.

In 1635 the decision was taken to remove the Knelle Dam on the Western side of Oxney and allow the Rother to take its natural course and once again flow in a southerly direction. This effectively was the death knell of boat building at Small Hythe and Reading Street as the water surrounding Oxney began to silt up as a result of the dissipation of the Rother.

Mithraic Alter piece - Stone church

When Oxney was an Island there had been three ferries operating from the mainland of Sussex and Kent to the Island, from Small Hythe and, Appledore on the Kent side and Maytham from the Sussex side for which tolls were charged. When the Rother silted up the ferries were replaced by bridges and the tolls continued for crossing these until 1936, although barges plied between Rye and Small Hythe, along the still navigable channel until 1924. So Igglesden would have paid a charge when he crossed the bridge onto the Island from Kent at the Ferry Inn at Stone, which was also the Toll House.

Today the Ferry Inn is a very popular hostelry, with not only locals, but also curious visitors, because as well as serving excellent food and an

The Ferry Inn, Stone

excellent choice of real ales it still displays on its front wall, by the entrance to the Inn, the scale of Toll charges. 1s-0d for a car or tractor, charabanc 1s-6d, Pigs 1d each, Foot Passenger 1/2d, Bath Chair 1d and so on.

You can best appreciate that Oxney was once an island, when approaching Rye station from Ashford on the railway across Romney Marsh. Looking to your right there, rising Xanadu like, from the Marsh, complete with cliff face, is what was clearly an Island.

Toll Charges at Ferry Inn

It's one of the features of this wonderful journey across the so called fifth continent. This appellation was attached to Romney Marsh by the Revd Richard Barham in his "Ingoldsby Legends", written in the 1800s.

Having put Oxney and Ebony into historical context its time now to examine Oxney's three villages in more detail and compare them today with 1923 when Igglesden visited over 100 years ago.

Igglesden's point of entry onto the island was over the Stone Ferrybridge and, after paying the appropriate Toll charge, he proceeded along what he calls the idyllic walk to Wittersham, its twisting lanes, with fields of hops and wheat on either side. Sadly hops are no longer grown on Oxney due to cheaper imports from Europe and a general change in drinking habits, a revolution in fact, when in the late 1960s lager began to take hold and now dominates the market. All that remains are the ubiquitous Oast houses where hops were dried, which are now converted into domestic dwellings or offices.

On reaching the crossroads at The Stocks and continuing over, there he tells us about the impressive white sailed Post Mill and it's equally impressive Mill House, which had been renovated by the famous actor Norman Forbes Robertson, shortly before Igglesden's visit. It is pleasing to report that both are still in excellent condition. As you enter Wittersham on the right you find that Igglesden's much lauded hostelry, The Ewe and Lamb, is also now a private dwelling house. Two doors down you

The Stocks, Post Mill

Ewe and Lamb pub, now a domestic dwelling

Le Neve

find the quirky village store called Neves, which at the time of Igglesden's visit had been operated for over 300 years by a Huguenot family by the name of Le Neve . Today like so many village shops it has ceased trading in the face of competition from the supermarkets. It is now an antique shop and charming dwelling house.

Directly opposite the old shop is Wittershams main thoroughfare, The Street. Further down The Street on the left is Wittersham Court, the

Wittersham Court, once Wittersham Manor

Wittersham House

site of the ancient manor house unchanged since Igglesden's time. Opposite a more recent construction, but nevertheless grade II listed, is Wittersham House which was redesigned by Edwin Lutyens early last century but more recently has been divided into luxury apartments surrounded by beautifully landscaped gardens.

In The Street there are many timber framed buildings, so typical of Wealden villages mostly covered by tiles, bricks or weather boarding. The

Typical timber framed tile-covered house

John the Baptist Church, Wittersham

main feature of The Street is the church of St John the Baptist which has one of the most beautiful church towers in Kent. Igglesden then goes on to describe in great detail the main features of the church. Being a member of the Kent Archaeological Society he had become an authority on church architecture.

Today, as is the usual practice, in the case of churches with their falling congregations, it is part of a benefice consisting of nine churches in the Tenterden area, under the capable Rectorship of The Rt. Revd Lindsay Hammond.

One omission on the part of Igglesden is the Swan Inn on the outskirts of Wittersham. Once a hostelry playing host to the local hunt. It had recently been taken over by new owners and given a facelift. It was the meeting place for the Wittersham Hunt.

A mile from the western end of Wittersham, is a railway station, Wittersham Road Station on the Kent and East Sussex Railway line from Tenterden, soon to be extended from Bodiam Castle to Robertsbridge.

Swan Inn and the hunt 1997

55

In his 1923 essay Igglesden fails to mention a now legendary event that took place in Wittersham in 1834 involving Wittersham Cricket Club. At this time the team was almost unbeatable and whilst celebrating yet another win the Landlord of the local Inn, the old Ewe and Lamb, growing tired of their boasting exclaimed "You can't play cricket, I can get two men who can beat the lot of you".

Idyllic Stone Cricket Club ground

The challenge was duly taken up and the Landlord produced two cricketers from nearby Benenden, Richard Mills and Ned Wenham who both played for Kent County .The game took place over two days on the 24th and 25th of September 1834 on the picturesque cricket ground next to the church watched by over 2000 people. Wenham and Mills scored 150 in their first innings before, Wenham was dismissed and bought the Benenden duos innings to a close "one out all out". Wittershams eleven were dismissed for only 55 in their first innings. In their second innings the Benenden pair scored 48 before Mills was caught on the boundary. Wittersham requiring 143 to win were dismissed for just 77. Sadly the villagers took the defeat badly and boycotted the local hostelry and within three years the Landlord was bankrupt

In 1936 Major Neve and others had the bright idea of reviving memories of the 1834 game by staging a return match. It was duly arranged for the 11th September 1936. The two professionals who made up the opposition were Bill Ashdown of Kent County Cricket Club and Bert Wensley of Sussex County Cricket Club appropriate since Wittersham was on the boundary of the two counties. This time it was to be a single innings.

What a tense situation; one slip on the part of the duo early on, and the game would be over. Over 3000 spectators turned up plus the BBC and the national press and interestingly The Kentish Express and its editor none other than Sir Charles Igglesden reporting under the sobriquet of LBW. Clearly making up for his omission of 1923. This time the game was a much closer affair, Wittersham scoring 153, which Ashdown and Wensley surpassed in just over two hours. Igglesden declared that as a Man of Kent he was proud of the performance of The Men of Oxney. Wittersham Cricket Club is still going strong today. So also is Stone in Oxney Cricket Club who play on one of the most picturesque grounds in Kent and after the game visit the Ferry Inn nearby to rehydrate.

It is hard to conceive that Oxney are World Champions of one of the oldest sports in the world and an Olympic sport until 1920, Tug of War. The team was formed at the Ewe and Lamb Public House in 1967. In 1975 Doug Reed, a Sussex farmer from Vine Cross, assisted by Sam Rolfe changed their name to Oxney/Vine Cross Tug of War Team and turned them into world beaters. Between, 1977-2001 they were virtually unbeatable, winning some 93 trophies worldwide as World Champions three times and European Champions once, each time representing England.

The Isle of Oxney Tug-of-War team 1971/72

Departing from Wittersham via The Swan we retrace our steps down to the euphoniously named hamlet Stone cum Ebony a place which has an air of mystery, all centring on its location on a cliff edge overlooking Romney Marsh which until the 13th century would have had the sea beating against its cliff face. That is, until reclamation took place all across Romney Marsh and associated areas in East Sussex.

The central feature architecturally is its 15th century church dedicated to St Mary the Virgin. Situated on the high ground above the cliff edge. It has wonderful

St Mary's Church, Stone

Far reaching views from St Mary's churchyard

views to both the north looking across the Weald towards the North Downs and to the south towards Rye Harbour, encompassing Romney Marsh on the Kent side and Fairlight on the Sussex side.

Since Igglesden's time two relics from the past have appeared in the church. First of all the Mithraic altar piece which had been situated in the vicarage garden when Igglesden visited in 1923, but in 1926 it was brought back into the church, where it had originally been up until 1721. At that time, because it was a pagan symbol it was banished from the church, and for 150 years was used as mounting block for horseman using the Black Ox Inn (Later renamed the Ferry Inn). Then 50 years later a more enlightened clergyman, the Revd William Gosling had it repaired and placed in the Vicarage garden. Then in 1926 the Parochial Church Council chairman, Mr G Lander DSc decided to bring the altar piece in from the cold and justified his actions as being to demonstrate the triumph of Christianity over paganism

The other relic from the past that appeared in the church after Igglesden's visit was even older than the altar piece, in fact 70 million years older. Housed in a 15th century glass case there were two relics, nine sections of the fossilised tail of an Iguanodon. They were were discovered in 1936 by a Mr Gill in Stone Quarry (now a lake) which is on the Wittersham Road behind the eponymous Quarry Cottages. Unfortunately these old fossils were prey to bounty hunters who removed sections. Sometime after 1987 what remained of the Iguanodon was initially removed to the safe keeping of the Maidstone Museum but are now with the Beaney House of Art and Knowledge in Canterbury.

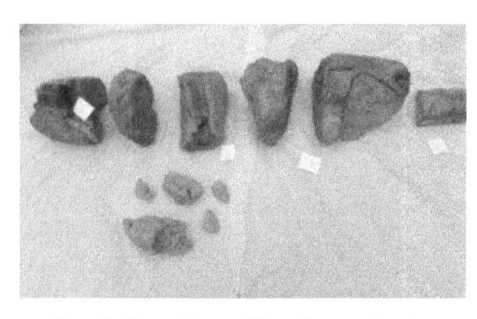

Fossils from Stone Church, now in the Beaney Museum in Canterbury

There still remains one point of the conjecture and that is the place of origin of the altar piece which experts have until recently maintained was carved in Lympne

As the stone is of a character common to that area. Archaeologist Andrew Richardson poses the question "Why would you carve such a piece in Lympne and then transport it to Oxney?" Far simpler to carve the stone locally. That begs the question of the possibility of a Roman Temple on Oxney. Andrew Richardson hypothesizes that there was a Roman Temple underneath the present church where bulls would be sacrificed on the altar piece and their carcasses shipped over to Small Hythe to continue the butchery process.

Historian and children's author Malcolm Saville certainly believed that there was a Roman Temple at Stone, in the grounds of the farm opposite Stone church, on the edge of the cliff. He incorporated this contention into his 1971 adventure story "Treasure at Amorys".

Finally if you are looking for the Stone village hostelry mentioned by Igglesden, The Crown, you will be disappointed. As you approach the village sign Stone Cum Ebony you see before you what appears to be the Crown Inn at the fork in the road. Alas it is now closed, having tried to become a haute cuisine style restaurant to appeal and attract customers beyond Oxney. It still continued to function as a bar serving ales in a very perfunctory way, but was not very welcoming in this guise, particulary to families, children were not welcomed in either the bar nor the restaurant. Falling between two stools it inevitably failed, like many others.

Old Crown Inn at Stone

Man of War at Reading Street deep water Channel

I have saved the most mysterious of this mystery strewn Island until last, the Island within an Island, Ebony, which Igglesden visited in 1900 and again in 1923.

To fully appreciate that Ebony really was a separate Island a trip down to the capacious Tenterden Garden Centre at Reading Street is required. Walking down from the garden centre on the A2080 and after

Former White Hart and Lamb Pub opposite former Toll House for Isle of Ebony

The crossing at Reading Sewer

about 50 yards you reach a right fork signposted Wittersham. In the centre of the fork is the former White Hart and Lamb hostelry, recently converted into a domestic dwelling. Opposite the former hostelry is a small dwelling which was the Toll House for the Isle of Ebony. Proceeding down the road to the bridge over the Reading Sewer you are about to cross over on to the Island of Ebony. Just before you cross over look up and there on the rising ground a mile distant is Chapel Bank the site of the Old Chapel and possibly the original village. The logic for such a location up on a plateau is easy to understand, because when it was truly an Island until the 17$^{th}$ century, the lower ground would, in winter, regularly flood.

Having crossed the bridge by Chapel Bank Farm, a trek across the fields steadily climbing to the summit is greatly rewarding for the views of the surrounding countryside. The Chapel Bank plateau is littered with worn gravestones bearing the name of many old Ebony families including those of Body, Packham, Paine, Ramsden and Poile (although most are now obliterated by weathering). However there is no church? That was removed in 1858 brick by brick and reconstructed in Reading Street opposite where the Tenterden Garden Centre now resides. Until 1801, this area had been part of The Civil Parish of Ebony.

St Mary's Church Ebony in situ on Chapel Bank Ebony before it was moved to its present location in 1858

Old Barrack Farm

Except for the boat building era the population of Ebony had been quite small about 160. There was however a brief period [1800-1815] when the population rose to about 350.This was due to the arrival of the army during the Napoleonic Wars. They were stationed around the Old Barracks Farmhouse, down by the Reading Sewer'. The church up on Chapel Bank suddenly became very busy with weddings, christenings and sadly many deaths from the Marsh Plague. The incidence of plague was, however greatly reduced by the building of The Royal Military Canal in 1806.

Drawing showing the much larger Elizabethan Church on Ebony.

The original church built on the Chapel Bank in about 850AD site was Saxon This was succeeded by a Norman church, which in 1210 was granted to Dover Priory, where it remained until the dissolution in 1535. Then in 1560 it was destroyed by a fire. A much smaller church was built which served the tiny parish until 1858, when it was

*Ebony Church now at Reading Street*

moved to Reading Street. However the church is now no longer on Ebony it had in reality followed its congregation. In 1882 a small school was built opposite the church on what today is the other side of the A2080, and is at the end of the Garden Centre car park. It is now an antique shop.

In 1958 to commemorate the centenary of St Mary's relocation a pilgrimage took place from Chapel Bank to Reading Street, led by the Archbishop of Canterbury Geoffrey Fisher. It has now become an annual

*Long Walk down Chapel Bank*

Rats Castle, Ebony home of the late Sir Donald Sinden

Gravestones left on Chapel Bank

event led by a distinguished ecclesiastical or a distinguished local resident. One year the actor Sir Donald Sinden CBE led the Pilgrimage, for he lived in Ebony for over 50 years, in a house called Rats Castle, on the Wittersham road, below Chapel Bank. In fact in 2014 when he died a tree was planted in his memory in the Chapel Bank graveyard, just as there had been for his son Jeremy when he died in 1996 and his wife Diana in 2004.

In addition to the Sindens another distinguished contemporary artist who lived on Oxney, at Stone, was George Newson the avant-garde composer who died in March 2024 aged 91. His speciality was electronic music in which form he composed concertos and operas. He was also a prolific photographer and many of his works are in The National Portrait Gallery.

As my journey through Oxney concludes, I am left with the sense that these two little hamlets of Stone and Ebony, possesses more mystique in their 5,600 acres than any other similar area of Kent. When you include the charms of Wittersham. The Isle of Oxney has to be one of the jewels in the Igglesden Saunters crown.

Milton Keynes UK
Ingram Content Group UK Ltd.
UKHW020353190924
448475UK00009B/61